The 9/11 Terrorist Attacks

THE HEROES OF 9/11
THEN AND NOW

Abdo & Daughters
MIDDLE GRADE NONFICTION

An imprint of Abdo Publishing
abdobooks.com

Jessica Rusick

ABDOBOOKS.COM

Published by Abdo Publishing, a division of ABDO, PO Box 398166, Minneapolis, Minnesota 55439. Copyright © 2021 by Abdo Consulting Group, Inc. International copyrights reserved in all countries. No part of this book may be reproduced in any form without written permission from the publisher. Abdo & Daughters™ is a trademark and logo of Abdo Publishing.

Printed in the United States of America, North Mankato, Minnesota.

102020

012021

THIS BOOK CONTAINS RECYCLED MATERIALS

Design: Kelly Doudna, Mighty Media, Inc.

Production: Mighty Media, Inc.

Editor: Liz Salzmann

Cover Photographs: Bebeto Matthews/AP Images (right), Shutterstock Images

Interior Photographs: Bebeto Matthews/AP Images, p. 1 (right); David J. Fenner/Wikimedia Commons, p. 9 (bottom); dpa picture alliance archive/Alamy, p. 12; ED BAILEY/AP Images, p. 22; EVAN VUCCI/AP Images, p. 17; Gene J. Puskar/AP Images, p. 33; Hubert Boesl/AP Images, pp. 4, 5; Jim Watson/Wikimedia Commons, pp. 30, 31, 45; John Munson/AP Images, p. 14; Kathy Willens/AP Images, p. 35; Library of Congress, pp. 36, 37; Mark Lennihan/AP Images, pp. 26, 27; R. D. Ward/Flickr, p. 34; Robert F. Bukaty/AP Images, p. 32; Sajeewashaluka/ Wikimedia Commons, p. 20; Shutterstock Images, pp. 1, 7, 18, 19, 24, 40, 41, 43, 44; Stephen Chernin/AP Images, p. 29; TSGT Cedric H. Rudisill, USAF/Wikimedia Commons, pp. 10, 11; US Army/Flickr, p. 21; US Army/Wikimedia Commons, p. 15; US Naval Academy/Wikimedia Commons, p. 9; US Navy/Wikimedia Commons, p. 16; White House/Flickr, pp. 13, 38

Design Elements: Shutterstock Images

LIBRARY OF CONGRESS CONTROL NUMBER: 2020940249

PUBLISHER'S CATALOGING-IN-PUBLICATION DATA

Names: Rusick, Jessica, author.

Title: The heroes of 9/11: then and now / by Jessica Rusick

Other title: then and now

Description: Minneapolis, Minnesota : Abdo Publishing, 2021 | Series: The 9/11 terrorist attacks | Includes online resources and index

Identifiers: ISBN 9781532194504 (lib. bdg.) | ISBN 9781098213862 (ebook)

Subjects: LCSH: September 11 Terrorist Attacks, 2001--Juvenile literature. | Acts of terrorism-- Juvenile literature. | Emergency medical personnel--Juvenile literature. | United States-- History--Juvenile literature.

Classification: DDC 363.3497--dc23

TABLE OF CONTENTS

The Twin Towers of the WTC collapsed after being hit by two airplanes.

Chapter 1

HEROES OF THE DAY

On September 11, 2001, the United States experienced the deadliest terrorist attack in its history. That day, terrorists hijacked four large commercial planes. They purposefully flew two planes into the Twin Towers of the World Trade Center (WTC) complex in New York City.

A third plane hit the Pentagon in Washington, DC, causing part of the building to collapse. A fourth plane crashed in a field in Pennsylvania. Officials believe this plane too was headed for a government building before it crashed.

Nearly 3,000 people died during these events. Of these, 2,753 victims were in New York City. The attack in Washington, DC, killed 184 victims, and 40 victims were killed in Pennsylvania. Together, these four crashes became known as the 9/11 terrorist attacks.

Heroes Take Action

The 9/11 terrorist attacks left the United States in shock. But heroes emerged amid the devastation. Stories of rescue, sacrifice, and kindness offered comfort and aid. And, as the United States rebuilt after the attacks, many more heroes offered helping hands.

Their sacrifices continue. Twenty years later, many survivors and rescuers still struggle with the physical and mental effects of the attacks. Memorials in New York CIty; Washington, DC; and Pennsylvania preserve their stories. And, these memorials ensure that future generations will never forget the heroes of September 11, 2001.

Heroes in the Air

The events of September 11 began in the skies. That morning, hijackers on four planes took control of the aircraft midflight. On American Airlines Flights 11 and 77 and United Airlines Flights 93 and 175, the hijackers forced passengers and crew to the backs of the planes. The hijackers threatened the passengers and crew with box cutters to make them follow orders.

On Flight 11, flight attendants Betty Ann Ong and Madeline "Amy" Sweeney used phones to report the hijacking to officials on the ground. They gave these officials important details, such as descriptions and the seat numbers of some of the hijackers. Similar calls were made from Flight 175 and Flight 77. This information would later help officials identify the terrorists through ticket records and discover what happened before the planes crashed.

Heroes on Flight 93

Passengers and crew members on Flight 93 used their cell phones and the in-flight phones to call ground crew and loved ones to report the hijacking. During these calls, those on the plane learned about the crashes at the WTC and the Pentagon. With shock, those aboard Flight 93 realized their plane was part of a larger attack.

Huddled in the back of the airplane, the passengers and crew took a vote. They decided to storm the cockpit and try to take back control of the plane. Flight attendant Sandy Bradshaw filled pitchers with hot water to use as weapons. On the phone with her husband, she said, "Everyone's running to first class. I've got to go."

People hung hats, photos, poems, signs, and more on a fence at the Flight 93 crash site to honor those who died there on 9/11.

WHO WERE THE HIJACKERS?

Within days of the attacks, US intelligence officials confirmed the hijackers were members of al-Qaeda. Al-Qaeda is an Islamist terrorist group. Its followers believe in enforcing strict laws based on an extreme interpretation of Islam. Al-Qaeda members often use violence to achieve this goal. People who follow Islam are called Muslims. Most Muslims do not agree with al-Qaeda's views. In fact, many Muslims think al-Qaeda's beliefs and actions go against the teachings of Islam.

Crash in Shanksville

Experts are not certain whether Flight 93's passengers and crew were able to break into the cockpit. The plane's cockpit had a voice recorder. Officials listened to the recording after the crash. They heard screams, shouts, and breaking glass. Whether the passengers and crew were in the cockpit or not, their actions alarmed the hijacker piloting the plane. To throw them off balance, he began to fly the plane sharply up and down. He also rolled the plane side to side.

When these actions did not stop the passengers and crew, the hijacker flew the plane at full speed into a field near Shanksville, Pennsylvania. All of Flight 93's passengers and crew died. However, their sacrifice may have saved lives. Experts believe the hijacker was planning to fly the plane into the White House or the US Capitol Building.

PIVOTAL PEOPLE: HEATHER "LUCKY" PENNEY AND MARC SASSEVILLE

Government officials thought Flight 93 could be heading for Washington, DC. Air National Guard pilots Heather "Lucky" Penney and Marc Sasseville were given a mission: stop Flight 93 before it reached the city. Penney and Sasseville quickly took off in their F-16 fighter jets to protect the capital. However, there had been no time to arm the jets before takeoff.

Heather "Lucky" Penney

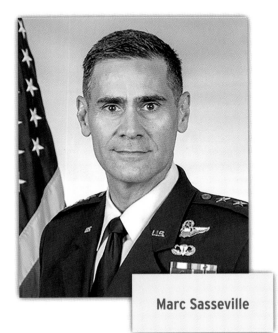

Marc Sasseville

That meant Penney and Sasseville would need to crash their jets into Flight 93 to stop it. Both pilots were prepared to do this. They would sacrifice their lives to prevent the plane from crashing into a building full of people. However, the two pilots did not have to do this. Flight 93 crashed in Pennsylvania before it reached Washington, DC.

The crash of Flight 77 caused a section of the west side of the Pentagon to collapse. Fuel from the plane exploded into flames, damaging much of the building near the crash site.

Chapter 2

RESCUES

When the two planes struck the WTC on September 11, there were an estimated 15,000 people in the Twin Towers. Most were office workers and businesspeople. They were not trained to handle anything like the situation they suddenly found themselves in.

The third plane was flown into the Pentagon in Washington, DC. The Pentagon is the headquarters of the US Department of Defense, so many of the people there were military personnel. But there were also civilian workers who did not have military defense training. Despite the fear, pain, and confusion, many people in both locations stepped up and became heroes that day.

North Tower Evacuations

Many people in the towers acted heroically simply by not panicking. Evacuations in both buildings were orderly, with little shouting or shoving. People felt that by staying calm, they could help others stay calm. As evacuations continued, many offered words of kindness and comfort to strangers. Evacuees also helped one another.

In the North Tower, office workers Michael Benfante and John Cerqueira carried Tina Hansen, a wheelchair user, down 68 flights of stairs to safety. Francis "Frank" De Martini and Pablo Ortiz, who also had offices in the North Tower, cleared blocked stairwells and freed people trapped by piles of debris. It is estimated the two men saved 50 people before they both lost their lives in the North Tower's collapse.

In 2011, Benfante released a memoir titled *Reluctant Hero*. In it, he discusses his experiences on 9/11 and how that day affected his life.

South Tower Rescues

As evacuations took place in the North Tower, officials instructed people in the South Tower to remain inside. At that point, most people assumed the first crash was an accident. Few imagined there could be a second plane crash. So, it seemed unnecessary to evacuate people from the South Tower.

However, financial company Morgan Stanley's head of security Rick Rescorla felt differently. A former army officer, Rescorla had

In 2019, Rescorla was awarded the Presidential Citizens Medal for his actions on 9/11. President Donald Trump (*right*) presented the medal to Rescorla's widow, Susan.

made Morgan Stanley employees working in the South Tower practice safety drills for years. Now, those drills paid off.

Rescorla started evacuating the company's employees as soon as Flight 11 hit the North Tower. He encouraged people to sing songs to raise morale as they descended the stairs. Rescorla's early actions led to 2,700 people evacuating the South Tower. But Rescorla was not one of them. He died in the South Tower's collapse.

When Flight 175 struck the South Tower, people from other

companies and offices also began evacuating the building. During the evacuation, many more heroes rose to help people escape.

Welles Crowther was a 24-year-old banker on one of the highest floors of the South Tower. As he was evacuating, he encountered a group of injured and dazed office workers. It was smoky and difficult to see. However, Crowther managed to find a safe, undamaged staircase. He directed the group to this staircase and carried an injured woman down more than 15 flights of stairs. Then others helped her continue down as Crowther went back up to search for more survivors. He saved at least ten people on September 11.

In 2014, President Barack Obama (*right*) spoke at the opening of the 9/11 Memorial Museum in New York City. Ling Young (*left*), one of the people Crowther helped, and Alison Crowther (*center*), Crowther's mother, also spoke at the event.

But Crowther did not escape the tower himself. His body was recovered from the wreckage six months after the attacks.

Not all rescuers lost their lives in the Twin Towers evacuations. On the eighty-fourth floor of the South Tower, Brian Clark felt the building sway from the impact of the plane. He started down the stairs. When he reached the eighty-first floor, he heard a voice. It belonged to Stanley Praimnath, who had been nearly eye level with Flight 175 as it struck the building. Praimnath was surrounded by loose wires and debris. Clark dug Praimnath out and pulled him to safety. The two escaped the South Tower together. Meanwhile, more than 230 miles (370 km) away, a third plane would soon strike in Washington, DC.

Patricia Horoho is credited with helping more than 75 people injured in the attack. She was later promoted to lieutenant general and served as the Surgeon General of the United States Army from 2011 to 2015.

Heroes at the Pentagon

At 9:37 a.m., Flight 77 crashed into the first floor of the Pentagon. Everyone inside the plane and 125 people in the building were

Medical personnel treat survivors of the Pentagon attack in a triage area near the building.

killed instantly. Hundreds of others were suddenly surrounded by fire and smoke.

As Pentagon employees struggled to escape, many of them stopped to help others. Navy Lieutenant Commander David Tarantino and Captain David Thomas lifted a pile of rubble off retired Navy commander Jerry Henson, freeing him just before part of the ceiling caved in. Both men survived. Sergeant Roxanne Cruz-Cortez and Corporal Eduardo Bruno carried their coworker's two-month-old baby to a nearby window, helping the mother, child, and several other workers escape to safety.

Army nurse Lieutenant Colonel Patricia Horoho felt her office in the Pentagon shake when Flight 77 hit. Outside, she saw many wounded people wandering in a daze. So, Horoho set up a triage area. She directed wounded people to a grassy area away from the crash site. There, Horoho helped treat survivors suffering from severe cuts, burns, and smoke inhalation.

Pentagon tour guide Beau Doboszenski was a former volunteer firefighter who had also trained as an emergency medical technician (EMT). He helped treat survivors at a triage station. He then joined a rescue team. This team went into the burning Pentagon to search for more survivors.

People who happened to be nearby also stepped in to help. Eric M. Jones was driving near the Pentagon when he saw the airplane crash into the building. He stopped his car and ran to help those in the building evacuate. Steve A. DeChiaro was walking outside the building when the plane hit. He also immediately went to the crash site to help. Both men carried people to safety and helped injured survivors find medical treatment. Jones and DeChiaro continued volunteering at the Pentagon for the next three days. They helped clear debris and recover bodies of those killed in the attack.

On July 15, 2002, Jones (*left*) and DeChiaro received the Secretary of Defense Medal of Valor. The medal recognizes acts of heroism in the face of danger.

Firefighters working at the WTC

Chapter 3

FIRST RESPONDERS

As office workers were helping one another evacuate on September 11, teams of emergency and rescue professionals also sprang into action. Within minutes of the Twin Towers being hit, New York City's 911 operators were flooded with calls. Dozens of calls were made by people inside the towers, including people who were trapped on floors near or above the crash sites.

The city's 911 operators were trained to respond to emergency situations, including fires in high-rise buildings. However, nothing had prepared them for the 9/11 terrorist attacks. At first, the operators did not have full information about what was going on at the WTC. They didn't know which floors the planes hit or that people had been told to evacuate.

However, these operators did their best to help people amid the confusion. They wrote down the locations of people and shared the information with rescue workers. They advised callers as best they could. And, they comforted those who were scared and grieving.

A VICTIM'S MESSAGE

Melissa Doi called 911 after she became trapped on the eighty-third floor of the South Tower. Over 24 minutes, Doi's 911 operator comforted her as she struggled to breathe in the smoke and heat. Doi gave the operator her mother's name and phone number. She asked the operator to deliver a message if Doi didn't make it out alive. Doi died in the South Tower's collapse. On the evening of September 11, the operator called Doi's mother to deliver her message: "Tell my mother that I love her and that she's the best mom in the whole world."

Police Officers and Firefighters

Following the North Tower attack, dozens of police officers and firefighters quickly arrived at the WTC complex. Many were on duty and called to the scene by dispatchers taking emergency calls. Others were off duty. However, when they saw the smoke and fire pouring from the towers, they felt the urge to help.

At the WTC, police officers and firefighters helped direct survivors

The 9/11 Memorial at Ground Zero has two pools with the 9/11 victims' names inscribed around them. Doi's name is etched on the side of the south pool.

safely out of the buildings and to nearby triage sites. Several responders risked getting hit by falling debris to help injured people on the plaza outside the towers. Meanwhile, other police officers and firefighters entered the Twin Towers. They searched floors for survivors, guiding them to stairwells and exits.

In the process of helping others escape, many firefighters and police officers lost their lives. Firefighters Orio J. Palmer and Ronald P. Bucca climbed to the plane's crash site on the seventy-eighth floor of the South Tower. They began planning how

In 2009, Bucca's daughter, Jessica Bucca-Hughes (*left*), and widow, Eve Bucca, received a US flag that once flew over a US military camp in Iraq that had been named in Bucca's honor.

to put out fires and evacuate injured people there. But at 9:59 a.m., the South Tower collapsed before they could carry out their plan.

Port Authority Police Department (PAPD) captain Kathy Mazza was also helping people in the South Tower. She was leading a group of survivors through its lobby when the building began to collapse. Mazza fired her weapon at the lobby's glass walls and doors, allowing many people to make a quick escape through the broken glass. But Mazza did not escape herself. She died in the collapse.

Peter J. Ganci Jr. was at a command post just outside the Twin Towers, coordinating the rescue efforts. Ganci was Chief of Department at the Fire Department of the City of New York (FDNY). When the South Tower collapsed, he and some of his men took shelter in the basement of a nearby building. They then had to dig their way through the rubble to resume their mission. Ganci was back at his command post when the North Tower collapsed at 10:28 a.m. More than 1,600 people were killed, including Ganci.

Prior to the North Tower collapse, six members of the FDNY

A year before the 9/11 terrorist attacks, Ganci (*right*), along with Fire Commissioner Thomas Von Essen (*left*) and New York City mayor Rudolph "Rudy" Giuliani (*center*) had cut the ribbon opening a new firehouse in the Bronx, New York.

had been told to evacuate it. On their way out, they came across office worker Josephine Harris. She was exhausted and injured and needed help down the stairs. Helping Harris slowed the firefighters' exit, but they refused to leave her. On the fourth floor, Harris slumped to the ground. She could go no farther.

That's when the building collapsed. Miraculously, they all survived. The firefighters comforted and cared for Harris until rescuers came to help the group out of the rubble. The firefighters later said that Harris saved them as much as they saved her. The stairs on the floors above and below them were crushed in the collapse.

2001 VS. TODAY

The 9/11 terrorist attacks identified issues with the emergency communications systems used by first responders. During the attacks, dispatchers were not set up to communicate directly with police and fire departments. And, police and fire departments did not have a shared radio system through which they could communicate. These issues made it more difficult to coordinate a response to the attacks.

In 2018, the US government and telecommunications company AT&T launched FirstNet. This is a nationwide network that first responders can use to communicate during crises. Today, FirstNet continues to expand across the United States.

If she hadn't stopped where she did, Harris and the firefighters likely would have died.

Though the city's firefighters and police officers rescued many people, it was a deadly day for both forces. In total, 343 firefighters and 60 police officers died in New York City on September 11.

Paramedics

New York paramedics arrived at the WTC to treat survivors. They set up triage areas around the complex. Many paramedics were hurt or

Since 2006, a firehouse across from the WTC site has featured a memorial wall honoring the 343 firefighters who died in the 9/11 terrorist attacks.

killed while helping others. For example, paramedic Manuel Delgado was injured by a wave of pressure caused by the South Tower's collapse, throwing him to the ground. Still, he walked on an injured ankle to a nearby ferry station to set up a new triage site. Other paramedics were injured or killed by falling debris and bodies.

9/11 BY THE NUMBERS

New York City's 911 operators received 57,000 calls during the 24 hours after the crashes. More than 3,000 of them were in the first 18 minutes after the North Tower was hit. About 130 of the calls came from inside the towers.

At triage sites, paramedics helped treat evacuees and first responders with serious injuries. These included severe burns and wounds from falling debris. Ambulances were standing by to take survivors to local hospitals. Normally, an ambulance carries one patient at a time. But that day, paramedics loaded the emergency vehicles with four or five patients at once to transport people more quickly.

At nearby hospitals, medical personnel quickly organized to treat survivors. Some hospital waiting rooms were crowded with people covered in gray dust from the Twin Towers' collapses. Many patients were treated for burns and smoke inhalation. The heroic actions of medical personnel and paramedics helped save and heal countless survivors of the attacks.

The collapse of the towers damaged or destroyed four subway stations and 1,200 feet (366 m) of train track.

Chapter 4

UNSUNG HEROES

Emergency and medical personnel, office workers, and even passersby helped people escape the 9/11 crash sites. But countless others did their part to help as well. Many of these helpers often go unrecognized.

As hundreds of first responders were called to action, many bus drivers brought them to the WTC. Subway workers sprang into action too. They dealt with hundreds of confused or upset passengers to shut down and evacuate subway stations.

One reason for shutting down the subway was the concern that the system could be used in further attacks. Also, the subway stations and tunnels near the WTC were damaged by the force of the towers falling. In some places, the tunnels and had caved in. In the weeks following September 11, New York City transit workers also helped rebuild portions of the subway that had been damaged.

In addition to closing the subway, officials closed many of the city's bridges and tunnels to traffic to protect the area from possible further attacks. At 11:02 a.m. on September 11, New York City mayor Rudolph "Rudy" Giuliani ordered the downtown area of Manhattan surrounding the WTC be evacuated. Manhattan is one of the five boroughs that make up New York City. Manhattan is an island surrounded by three rivers.

With many of the bridges and tunnels leading off the island shut down, people had fewer ways to evacuate. Local mariners came to the rescue. Ferries, police boats, Coast Guard vessels, and other craft pulled up to the city's riverbanks. Throughout the day, 800 mariners in 150 boats helped thousands of people evacuate.

After the area around the WTC was evacuated, the city's sanitation workers started clearing away rubble. They made paths through the debris at the WTC so first responders could continue rescue efforts. In the weeks following the attacks, sanitation workers also removed rotting food and other garbage from nearby empty buildings. And, they sorted through WTC debris at a landfill in Staten Island, New York, separating out human remains and artifacts from the wreckage of the buildings.

Canine Heroes

Humans were not the only heroes on 9/11. Sales manager Michael Hingson was working on the seventy-eighth floor of the North Tower when the first plane hit. He is blind and depended on his guide dog, Roselle, to guide him out of the building. The pair left the North Tower just as the South Tower fell. Even as debris rained down, Roselle stayed calm, leading Hingson out of the building and

to safety at a nearby subway station.

Other canine heroes emerged in the days following the attacks. More than 300 search and rescue dogs sniffed the rubble at the WTC, searching for survivors. One was a former police dog named Trakr. Trakr's handler, James Symington, had driven 14 hours from Canada to help after the attacks.

Early in the morning on September 12, Trakr picked up the scent of WTC office worker Genelle Guzman-McMillan. Guzman-McMillan was alive, but she had been pinned beneath the rubble for 27 hours. She was the last survivor recovered from the WTC.

Dogs also helped first responders and survivors cope with trauma. At the WTC, therapy dogs comforted workers as they took breaks from digging through the rubble. And across New York, therapy dogs comforted and soothed survivors and others who sought counseling after the attacks.

Rescue workers use buckets to clear debris as they search for survivors.

Chapter 5

HEROES IN THE AFTERMATH

September 11, 2001, was just the first day heroes stepped up. People from many backgrounds helped in the following days, weeks, and months in New York City; Washington, DC; and Pennsylvania. These workers and volunteers quickly began cleaning, rebuilding, and helping attack survivors recover.

Ground Zero

In New York City, the wreckage of the WTC complex became known as Ground Zero. The site was 16 acres (6 ha) of mangled steel beams, broken concrete and glass, and other debris. Fires continued to burn beneath the rubble for 100 days.

Volunteers from New York and around the country came to help at Ground Zero. These heroes included police officers, firefighters, and paramedics. In the days after the attacks, they

combed through the wreckage by hand for survivors. Many worked for more than 12 hours at a time. Fewer than 20 people were found alive and rescued.

Professional personnel weren't the only people working at Ground Zero. Some volunteers served food and passed out water to those working at Ground Zero. Others, like Sister Cynthia Mahoney, served as counselors to Ground Zero workers. Talking to counselors helped workers deal with the trauma of continually finding dead bodies in the wreckage. Mahoney also comforted friends and relatives of victims who came to visit the site where their loved ones died. And she performed Christian religious blessings over the remains of victims.

At times, there were more volunteers than officials could accommodate. Although not every volunteer was needed, the long lines showed just how many people were willing to lend a hand.

Pennsylvania & Washington, DC

In Pennsylvania and Washington, DC, workers and volunteers worked tirelessly as well. In Pennsylvania, hundreds of volunteers, emergency responders, and others helped gather airplane parts from the field where Flight 93 crashed. Workers also marked any debris that could be human remains. These were then collected by specialists

Investigators search the Flight 93 crash site in Pennsylvania for the plane's voice recorder and other evidence that could provide information about what happened during the hijacking.

The day after the attacks, firefighters and military personnel hung a large US flag on the Pentagon next to the damaged area. The flag symbolized the strength and resilience of the American people.

who worked to identify the victims. Final sweeps of the site were completed on September 30. Over the following three days, a restoration team finished the cleanup.

Meanwhile at the Pentagon, parts of the building were not damaged. Maintenance crews ensured that these areas were safe and that the electricity and plumbing were working properly. The day after the attacks, office workers returned to these portions of the building.

In October, workers began to clear away the damaged areas of the Pentagon. On November 19, reconstruction officially began. The goal was to complete the reconstruction by the one-year anniversary of the attacks. Crews worked seven days a week in twelve-hour shifts. They finished the project in August 2002, four weeks ahead of schedule.

Restoration

While workers wrapped up the main cleanup of the Washington, DC, and Pennsylvania sites within a couple months of the attacks, the WTC saw more than eight months of continued cleanup efforts. Full-time workers at the site included ironworkers, carpenters, and heavy equipment operators. For months, these heroes worked grueling 20-hour shifts, leaving only to shower and sleep. They preserved human remains and personal effects found in the wreckage, fought fires, and cleared away rubble and damaged structures. The work was physically and emotionally exhausting for many.

Due to the dedication of these hundreds of heroes, Ground Zero cleanup was finally finished in May 2002. This was months sooner than expected. Workers had cleared 1.8 million tons (1.6 million t) of debris from the site.

The final large piece of the WTC to be removed was a steel support column from the South Tower.

Some first responders working at the 9/11 terrorist attack sites were overcome with emotion.

Chapter 6

ONGOING CHALLENGES

After the attacks, many 9/11 heroes faced unique challenges. Some suffered from mental illnesses such as post-traumatic stress disorder (PTSD). Some people with 9/11-related PTSD found it impossible to return to work. Others continued to have nightmares about the horrors they witnessed. And, for many, certain sounds and sights triggered memories of September 11. These challenges were enduring. In 2019, at least 10,000 civilians and first responders were being treated for 9/11-related PTSD.

Effects of Air Pollution

Illnesses related to breathing the air at Ground Zero became another challenge for those who worked at the site. When the Twin Towers fell, their building materials as well as their contents were crushed. Tiny particles from this debris were released into the air. These particles contained dangerous substances such as asbestos, lead, and silica.

However, officials weren't clear about the

danger of breathing the air around Ground Zero. So, workers often did not wear protective masks. Many cleanup workers as well as those who survived the attacks were initially treated for coughing and trouble breathing. For many people, these problems developed into long-term respiratory and digestive illnesses or cancer.

Congress Takes Action

In 2001, the US Congress created the September 11th Victim Compensation Fund (VCF). From 2001 to 2004, the fund gave money to people who were physically injured in the attacks. This helped them pay for medical bills and other expenses. The VCF also gave money to the families of victims. By 2011, however, it was clear that many first responders were continuing to become sick from 9/11-related illnesses. So, Congress reactivated the fund that year and then renewed it in 2015 to continue helping to pay for their medical care.

The VCF's 2011 reactivation was part

In 2019, Congress passed a bill to make the September 11th Victim Compensation Fund permanent. President Trump signed it on July 29, 2019.

of the James Zadroga 9/11 Health and Compensation Act of 2010. The bill was named for James Zadroga, a New York City police officer who spent weeks working at Ground Zero. Zadroga's health got continually worse after his exposure to the air at the site. He died in 2006. In addition to reactivating the VCF, the Zadroga Act created the World Trade Center Health Program. This program treats those with physical or mental illnesses caused by the 9/11 terrorist attacks.

Toll on New York Fire and Police Departments

Another challenge after 9/11 was rebuilding the firefighting and police forces of New York City. September 11, 2001, was the deadliest day in history for US police officers and firefighters. The FDNY lost many of its most experienced firefighters. Those losses continued as more police officers and firefighters got sick after breathing the air at Ground Zero.

The PAPD launched a massive hiring effort after 9/11. This was both to replace officers it lost and to increase its security capabilities. The PAPD is the police department of the Port Authority, which manages the WTC complex and other facilities. Today, the force has 2,300 officers, nearly twice as many as in 2001.

The FDNY updated its training programs to help less experienced recruits take the places of those who died. Today, some of these recruits include the children of firefighters who died at the WTC. In 2019, 13 children of New York firefighters killed on 9/11 graduated from the FDNY Training Academy. Six others were the children of firefighters who died from 9/11-related illnesses.

The Tower of Voices structure was completed in 2018. The wind chimes were installed over the next couple of years.

Chapter 7

HONORING 9/11 HEROES

Over the years, the heroes of 9/11 have been honored with medals, ceremonies, and memorials. In 2002, Congress approved a national memorial at the site of the Flight 93 crash in Pennsylvania. The memorial includes the Wall of Names, which lists the passengers and crew members. It also features the Tower of Voices. This tower is 93 feet (28 m) tall and includes 40 wind chimes. Each chime represents one of the victims who were on Flight 93.

On June 15, 2006, construction began on a 9/11 memorial at the Pentagon. It opened to the public on September 11, 2008. The Pentagon Memorial includes 184 benches that each extend over a small pool of water. The pools are lit up at night. Each bench has the name of a person who died in the attack at the Pentagon.

Ground Zero

The 9/11 terrorist attacks are commemorated in New York City as well. Every September 11, a special ceremony is held at Ground Zero.

During the ceremony, family members of the victims take turns reading aloud the names of those who died on 9/11.

On September 9, 2005, President George W. Bush awarded a 9/11 Heroes Medal of Valor to all public safety officers killed in the attacks. The heroes' families attended the ceremony. Bush told these families, "Your loved ones will always have the thanks and admiration and respect of a grateful nation."

The 9/11 Memorial & Museum

On September 11, 2011, a memorial was dedicated at Ground Zero. The 9/11 Memorial features two large pools where the Twin Towers once stood. The names of those who died in the 9/11 terrorist attacks are inscribed around the pools.

In May 2014, the 9/11 Memorial Museum opened at Ground Zero. Its collection includes hundreds of stories from survivors. It also features objects that reflect the heroism of the day. These include a badly damaged fire truck and leather gloves worn by a Ground Zero worker.

The Memorial Glade was added to the 9/11 Memorial in 2019. The glade's large stones are arranged along a path next to the south pool.

9/11 BY THE NUMBERS

When the 9/11 Memorial Museum opened, it contained 12,500 9/11-related objects, 1,995 stories of survivors and witnesses, and 580 hours of film and video.

The Memorial Glade commemorates those who have gotten sick or died from 9/11-related illnesses in the years following the attacks.

Many who visit the 9/11 Memorial & Museum leave behind tributes to 9/11 heroes and lost loved ones. These include letters, stuffed animals, and photos. These items are collected nightly by museum staff and stored in the museum.

Forever Heroes

The world is much different today than it was on September 11. The crash sites have been cleared and rebuilt. Memorials have been erected. Through these memorials and the stories from survivors and witnesses, the courage and bravery of 9/11's heroes live on. Their actions can inspire us to act selflessly not just in crises, but in everyday life. On the twentieth anniversary of the 9/11 terrorist attacks, it is important to remember these heroes. Their legacies will continue to be honored for many more years to come.

TIMELINE

8:46 A.M.
American Airlines Flight 11 strikes the North Tower of the WTC.

9:37 A.M.
American Airlines Flight 77 strikes the first floor of the Pentagon.

10:03 A.M.
United Airlines Flight 93 crashes in a field near Shanksville, Pennsylvania.

11:02 A.M.
Mayor Giuliani orders the evacuation of downtown Manhattan.

SEPTEMBER 11, 2001

9:03 A.M.
United Airlines Flight 175 the South Tower of the WTC.

9:59 A.M.
The South Tower collapses.

10:28 A.M.
The North Tower collapses.

Thank You America
For Your Prayers and Support For
All Those Lost And Their Families
From The Port Authority NY & NJ Police

SEPTEMBER 12, 2001
The last survivor is recovered from Ground Zero.
Some Pentagon workers return to their offices.

MAY 2002
Cleanup at Ground
Zero finishes.

OCTOBER 3, 2001
Cleanup and restoration
efforts end at the
Flight 93 crash site.

SEPTEMBER 9, 2005
President George W. Bush awards
a 9/11 Heroes Medal of Valor to
each public safety officer who
died in the 9/11 terrorist attacks.

SEPTEMBER 11, 2008
A 9/11 memorial is dedicated
at the Pentagon.

MAY 2014
The 9/11 Memorial
Museum opens at
Ground Zero.

SEPTEMBER 11, 2011
The 9/11 Memorial
is dedicated at
Ground Zero.

MAY 30, 2019
The Memorial Glade is dedicated
at the 9/11 Memorial. This addition
commemorates those affected
by 9/11-related illnesses.

GLOSSARY

artifact—an object remaining from a particular location or time period.

asbestos—minerals that builders once used to fireproof buildings. Today, scientists know that breathing in asbestos fibers can cause diseases such as cancer.

borough—one of five divisions of New York City. They are Manhattan, the Bronx, Queens, Brooklyn, and Staten Island.

civilian—of or relating to something nonmilitary. A civilian is a person who is not an active member of the military.

commemorate—to honor and remember an important person or event.

digestive—of or relating to the breakdown of food into simpler substances the body can absorb.

dispatcher—a person whose job is to send someone or something to a particular place for a particular purpose.

hijack—to take over by threatening violence.

inhalation—the act of breathing in.

Islam—the religion of Muslims as described in the Koran. Islam is based on the teachings of the god Allah through the prophet Muhammad.

landfill—a system used for garbage disposal. Trash is layered with earth to build up an area of land.

legacy—something important or meaningful handed down from previous generations or from the past.

memorial—something that serves to remind people of a person or an event.

morale—the enthusiasm and loyalty a person or group feels about a task or job.

paramedic—someone trained to care for a patient before or during the trip to a hospital.

post-traumatic stress disorder (PTSD)—a mental condition that can be caused by a very shocking or difficult experience. Symptoms of PTSD include depression and anxiety.

respiratory—having to do with the system of organs involved with breathing.

sanitation—related to keeping places free from dirt, infection, and disease by removing waste and trash.

therapy—relating to the treatment of diseases and disorders.

trauma—a wound or injury to the body or the mind.

triage—related to the process of deciding which patients should be treated first based on how sick or seriously injured they are.

ONLINE RESOURCES

Booklinks
NONFICTION NETWORK
FREE! ONLINE NONFICTION RESOURCES

To learn more about the heroes of 9/11, please visit **abdobooklinks.com** or scan this QR code. These links are routinely monitored and updated to provide the most current information available.

INDEX